Every Kid's Guide to
Using Time Wisely

Written by
JOY BERRY

GROLIER ENTERPRISES INC.
Danbury, Connecticut

About the Author and Publisher

Joy Berry's mission in life is to help families cope with everyday problems and to help children become competent, responsible, happy individuals. To achieve her goal, she has written over two hundred self-help books for children from birth through age twelve. Her work revolutionized children's publishing by providing families with practical, how-to, living skills information that was previously unavailable in children's books.

Joy gathered a dedicated team of experts, including psychologists, educators, child developmentalists, writers, editors, designers, and artists, to form her publishing company and to help produce her work.

The company, Living Skills Press, produces thoroughly researched books and audio-visual materials that successfully combine humor and education to teach subjects ranging from how to clean a bedroom to how to resolve problems and get along with other people.

Managing Editor: Ellen Klarberg
Copy Editor: Kate Dickey
Contributing Editors: Libby Byers, Maureen Dryden,
Yona Flemming, Gretchen Savidge
Editorial Assistant: Sandy Passarino

Art Director: Laurie Westdahl
Design: Abigail Johnston, Laurie Westdahl
Production: Abigail Johnston, Caroline Rennard
Illustrations designed by: Bartholomew
Inker: Linda Hanney
Colorer: Linda Hanney
Composition: Curt Chelin

Planning how you spend your time is one of the most important things you can do.

EVERY KID'S GUIDE TO USING TIME WISELY will help you learn about
- time,
- time management,
- yearly plans,
- monthly and weekly plans,
- daily plans, and
- following through with plans.

Time is when things happen.

Time can be measured by a clock.

A clock measures and shows seconds, minutes, and hours.

A calendar also shows time.
A calendar shows days, weeks, months, and years.

Time has a
- past (the time that has already happened),
- present (the time right now), and
- future (all the time to come).

Time never
- stops,
- slows down, or
- goes faster.

Everyone has the same amount of time in a day.

Everyone spends some time sleeping.

Everyone spends some time eating.

Most people spend some time at work or school.

Most people spend some time doing things that must be done.

Most people spend some time playing and relaxing.

You can figure out exactly how you spend your time. Begin by making two time charts.

Make **Time Chart 1.**

It should look something like this:

TIME CHART #1							
TIME	SUN.	MON.	TUE.	WED.	THUR.	FRI.	SAT.
12:00 - 6:00 A.M.							
6:00 - 7:00 A.M.							
7:00 - 8:00 A.M.							
8:00 - 9:00 A.M.							
9:00 - 10:00 A.M.							
10:00 - 11:00 A.M.							
11:00 - 12:00 A.M.							
12:00 - 1:00 P.M.							
1:00 - 2:00 P.M.							
2:00 - 3:00 P.M.							
3:00 - 4:00 P.M.							
4:00 - 5:00 P.M.							
5:00 - 6:00 P.M.							
6:00 - 7:00 P.M.							
7:00 - 8:00 P.M.							
8:00 - 9:00 P.M.							
9:00 - 10:00 P.M.							
10:00 - 12:00 P.M.							

Make **Time Chart 2.**

It should look something like this:

Here is how to use **Time Chart 1.**
Begin on a Sunday.

Take some time every day to write on the chart what you have done each hour.

For example: From midnight to seven o'clock on Sunday morning you were probably sleeping. So, write *sleeping* in each space that represents that time period.

Here is how to use **Time Chart 2.**

In the "activity" column, write each thing you did during the week. Add up the total hours you spent on each activity each day. Write each total in the space under "total hours spent each day."

Add up the total hours you spent on each activity all week. Write each total in the last column of the chart.

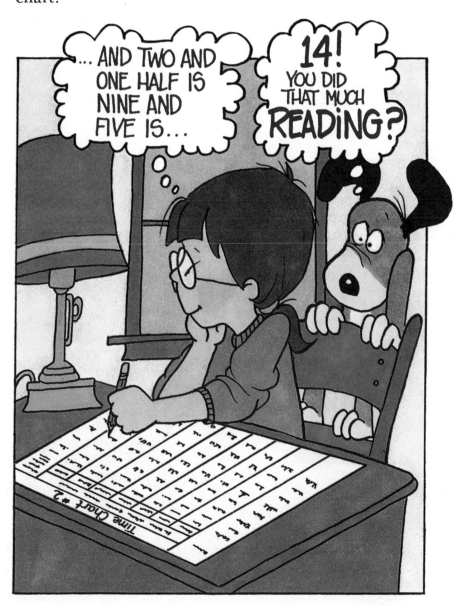

Study **Time Chart 2** by answering these questions:
- What did you spend the most time doing?
- What did you spend the least time doing?
- Is there something you would like to have spent more time doing?
- Is there something you would like to have spent less time doing?

- Is there something you didn't do that you would like to have done?
- Did you have enough free time to do whatever you wanted to do?
- Did you spend enough time doing the things you needed to do?
- Do you feel good about the way you spend your time?

If you are like most people your age, you probably spend a lot of time sleeping and attending school. This is time you *cannot* control.

However, you *can* control the time when you are not asleep or in school. You can use the remaining time to do whatever you need or want to do.

Some of the things you need or want to do can be done in a day. Some can be done in a week. Others require a month or a year.

Because this is true, you will need to have

- *yearly plans* for what you hope to accomplish during a year;
- *monthly plans* for what you hope to accomplish during a month;
- *weekly plans* for what you hope to accomplish during a week;
- *daily plans* for what you hope to accomplish during a day.

You will need these items to help you make your yearly, monthly, weekly, and daily plans:

- a large sheet of paper
- a calendar with spaces large enough to write in
- a tablet of blank paper
- a pencil
- an eraser

You might also want to have
- a clock and
- a watch.

The beginning of January is a good time to make yearly plans. So is the month that school begins. However, it is possible to make yearly plans anytime.

To make yearly plans you will need to ask yourself these questions:

Make a list. Write down your answers to the questions.

Study your list. Eliminate the things that are unimportant or impossible.

Carefully go over your list. Cross off anything you are not sure you want to do. Also cross off anything you won't be able to do.

Make a priority list. Decide which of the things that remain on your list are the most important. Decide which of the things are not so important.

Put the most important things at the top of the list and the least important things at the bottom.

Make a goal chart. The things you write on your priority list are your *goals.*

Use the large sheet of paper to make a chart of your goals. Put the chart in a place where you will see it every day. The chart will remind you of the things you want to accomplish during the year.

Much of what you do during a month or a week will depend on what your goals are.

To make your monthly and weekly plans, you will need to do the following:

- Think about your goals.
- Consider each goal.
- Ask yourself the question, "What do I need to do to accomplish this goal?"

Make a list. Write down everything you need to do
in order to achieve each goal.

Organize your list. Write down the things you need to do in the order in which they must be done.

Fill in your calendar. Write the following in the daily spaces of your calendar:

- the things you need to do to achieve your goals,
- the appointments you make for yourself, and
- the appointments you make with other people.

Be sure to use a pencil so you can erase if your plans should change.

Make a "things-to-do" list.
Keep your pencil and pad of paper handy. Anytime
you think of something you need or want to do,
write it down on your "things-to-do" list.

Check your calendar every morning. Add the things you are supposed to do that day to your "things-to-do" list.

Keep your "things-to-do" list up to date. When you do something, cross it off your list.

Check your list at the end of each day. Put the
things you have not crossed off at the top of your
"things-to-do" list for the next day.

Sometimes you might not want to do a task on your goal chart, calendar, or "things-to-do" list. But sometimes it is necessary to do things you do not want to do.

It will help if you avoid procrastinating, escaping, and breaking promises.

Avoid procrastinating.

Do not wait until later to do a job. Do it as soon as possible so you will have time to do the things you want to do.

Avoid escaping.

Do not try to get out of doing a task by doing something else. Focus your attention on the task that needs to be done until it is finished.

Avoid breaking promises.

Do not make promises you will not be able to keep.
Do not say you will do something and then neglect to
do it. Do what you say you will do.

There are things you can do to make an undesirable task easier to do.

Race with the clock.
Set a time limit for a task. Then try to get the job done in the allotted time or sooner.

Reward yourself.

Promise yourself you will do something you really want to do after you finish a task. Then keep the promise you make to yourself.

Planning how you spend your time is one of the most important things you can do because time is an important part of life.